Then & Now

EBBW VALE

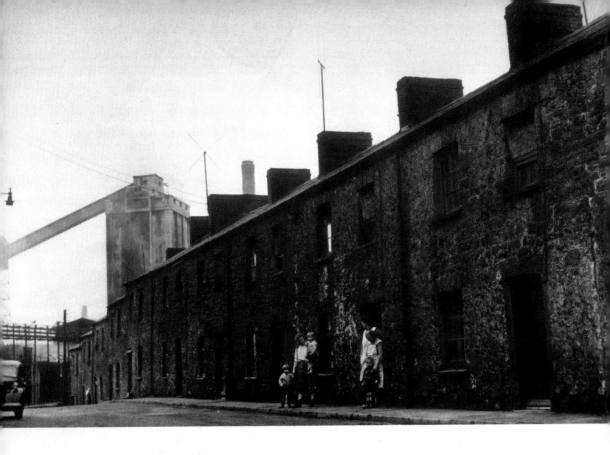

Lethbridge Terrace, built in the 1830s, was named after Sir Thomas Lethbridge of Bath, who founded the Victoria Ironworks in 1837. This terrace was adjacent to the Ebbw Vale steelworks and the coal bunker can be seen in this picture.

In the lower photograph a part of the New Hilltop housing estate, built in the 1950s, is shown. This estate was built to relocate the residents of Victorian style housing.

Then & Now
EBBW VALE

COMPILED BY IDWAL WILLIAMS
AND ALAN TUDGAY

TEMPUS

Tempus Publishing Limited
The Mill, Brimscombe Port,
Stroud, Gloucestershire, GL5 2QG

ISBN 0 7524 1652 9

Typesetting and origination by
Tempus Publishing Limited
Printed in Great Britain by
Midway Clark Printing, Wiltshire

A view looking south from Victoria Road towards the Ebbw Vale steelworks during the early 1900s. In the bottom left of the picture is the lower end of Victoria Road while Boundry Road, demolished in the 1950s, is on the right of the foreground. Victoria Colliery can be seen, along with Lethbridge Terrace and Bath Terrace.

CONTENTS

ACKNOWLEDGMENTS

I would like to extend my grateful thanks to the following local people who have shown their support by willingly loaning material for this book, and who have been a constant source of information and photographs. Thanks go especially to Alan Tudgay whose knowledge of the area and its people proved invaluable in gathering together the photographs of yesteryear.

Special thanks also go to: Blaenau Gwent Borough Council (Civic Collection), Mrs Barbara Thomas, Mrs Jean Hoskins, Mrs Barbara Evans, Mrs Florence Jones Mrs Catherine Richards, Dennis Jones, Keith Davies, Glyn Powell, Derek Harding, Terry Lewis, Stephen McKelvie, Jim Holland, Keith Jones, Eric Smith, Wyndham Morris, Bill Randell, David and Bob Clubb, Bob Hallett, Martin Henry, Roger Burchell, Elvet Poultney, Gareth Jenkins and Graham Jones.

I would also like to thank all of those who contributed material and photographs and regret that not all of it can be used in the book.

BIBLIOGRAPHY

History of Ebbw Vale	A. Gray-Jones
History of Ebbw Vale	F.J. Ball
Pictorial History of Ebbw Vale	F.J. Ball
Ebbw Vale in Old Photographs	K. Thomas
There's Rosemary	Monmouthshire Education Committee
The Past and Present History of Ebbw Vale	Charles Parry
Discover Ebbw Vale	Roger Burchill

INTRODUCTION

To the casual visitor Ebbw Vale may seem like any other valleys town, but the visitor soon becomes aware that the history and background of the town has bred a special group of people. People who are prepared to work for the common good of the community, without any thought of the cost to themselves.

In 1780, iron making came to Ebbw Vale and the town grew from being mainly agricultural, with twenty-nine farms and smallholdings on the eastern side of the valley and fifteen farms and smallholdings on the western side of the valley, to what it is today.

Since those early days the town has seen many changes in the fortunes of its people. From high employment and prosperity to the depression and poverty of the 1920s, Ebbw Vale has known both the highs and lows of the industrial age. When Winston Churchill famously said 'All I have to offer is Blood, Sweat and Tears' he could well have been thinking of the people of Ebbw Vale.

During the past 220 years there have been many lives lost and many workers injured in the often dangerous industries, such as coal mining or quarrying, which were necessary for the iron making to proceed.

Housing was one of the things that improved with the advent of iron making in the valley. Preservation of the community spirit was taken into account when old houses in an area were demolished. Friends and neighbours were all able to move en-bloc to a new housing site, preventing the break-up of communities.

It would appear however, that the wheel has again turned full circle. The steel industry in the valley is on the decline, and Ebbw Vale has now become more of a service area, supplying parts made mainly in small factory units to other service users.

Thankfully, our predecessors made provisions for the teaching and training of the young. They provided us with some excellent schools, such as the grammar school (although this is due to be demolished soon), the technical school and the various secondary, primary, junior and special schools in the town. In 1849, the first adult learning centre in the valley was set up in Penuel chapel, alongside the Sunday schools. After the Institute was built in 1853 and opened in 1854, the centre was transferred there before becoming a technical school. That in turn led to the North Gwent College being founded and later to become part of the Gwent Tertiary College.

Because the people worked hard and played hard, the end result was a community of super fit sportsmen and women, many of who have represented their country or played for various well-known sports clubs. Cwm, an outlying part of the town, has been blessed with an abundance of such gifted people.

The progress of Ebbw Vales has not been without its problems, with some of the iron masters more concerned with profits than the welfare of the workforce. This resulted in the Chartist Riots in 1839 that culminated in thousands of men marching to from the Monmouthshire Valleys to Newport to release the Chartist leaders who had been arrested for trying to improve working conditions. The riots have been well charted in books such as *The Rape of the Fair Country*. The Society of Friends, who fought to improve the conditions of the workers and their families, founded one of the first Trade unions in 1810 near the Rhyd y Blew. This was known as the The Beaufort and and Ebbw Vale United Society.

Looking through the book we will see how the town itself has improved over the years, largely thanks to the foresight of Ebbw Vale's forefathers.

As we take our tour through the town it may be easier if we start in the Victoria area and take a stroll with perhaps a short detour to places of interest. The route will take us along the western side of the valley to a point just beyond the leisure centre, then up to Beaufort for a brief visit before continuing down the eastern side of the valley. Here we will see the steel works, and take a quick peek at what became of the once thriving steel making in Ebbw Vale. We will then continue through Waunlwyd and the Garden Festival of Wales site, down to Cwm, before moving up the western side of the valley to our starting point. We can be proud of what we has been achieved on our behalf by our forefathers, even though, with the benefit of hindsight, we sometimes criticise and suggest that things could have been done better. If there is a community that has had to fight for what it now possesses it is Ebbw Vale. We can only hope to do for the future inhabitants of Ebbw Vale what has been done for us in the past.

Idwal Williams 1999

Perhaps the words of a poem by Catherine Richards (née Pugh) of Ebbw Vale would be most appropriate when it comes to describing the history of the town:

GLYN-EBBW

The fields were once all shining green
A living, changing, verdant sheen;
The valley sides were rich with trees
A-shimmer in the upland breeze;
The lime-washed farmsteads, staring white,
Gleamed friendly like kind lamps at night;
The moor-born stream in loud delight
Proclaimed its undisputed right
To run the meadows, woods and hedgerows
And shelter flashing trout and minnows,
Along the moor-land road raised high
Against the radiant blue, blue sky
Long lines of cream, soft woolly sheep
Made for the plain o'er scarpment steep,
With drovers lilting as they spoke

Laid waste the beauty of this glen.
They ripped the earth for coal and ore,
Stripped bare the hillside, scarred the moor,
Usurped the woods, the last brave tree,
By tips of monstrous symmetry,

And thrust long arms of sterile shale
Along the fertile shower-fresh vale
To choke the stream and kill the fish
As though with one consuming wish:
To see that no fair thing should thrive
In this black death-producing hive.
Cream flocks no more bespeck the green;
Some tattered remnants, grey and lean,
Eke out their life, uncherished band
Of raiders in their own homeland.

The valley's life gave way to wealth.
Two things survive as though by stealth:
The tongue which was the shepherds pride,
The tongue by which they lived and died;
The songs they sang in grief or joy,
The songs no changes can destroy.

May these treasures of a distant, prouder age
Keep us mindful of a fading heritage.

Chapter 1

VICTORIA ROAD

TO CHURCH STREET

The middle part of Victoria Road looking north towards Christ Church. Note the barbers pole and the style of clothes worn during the early 1900s. The houses on the left still remain.

Victoria Road was once the heart of the community, where all the necessities of life could be obtained without having to leave the street. Note the sides of bacon hanging outside the butcher's shop. As can be seen from the present day picture the site has been transformed into a pleasant green park-like area. The shops on the street are gone and the car has replaced the horse and cart. The street is known locally as the Gin Shop Hill after local alehouse The Victoria Hotel, known as The Gin Shop. It was demolished in 1972

The Palace Cinema, built in 1892 and originally known as the Central Hall, was situated just north of Victoria road and opposite Christ Church. The Palace, which at one time was able to seat 1,500, was host to many functions and performances by noted artists of the day. It was also used by workers from the steel works for their annual Christmas pantomime. Children of the workforce were admitted free to the pantomime and the show always proved popular with the youngsters. It was demolished in 1971 and the site today is used as a casual car park. The corner, with the gas lamp became known as 'penniless corner', owing to the number of unemployed people that used to congregate there, to pass the time away.

THE PALACE, Church St, Ebbw Vale.   M.J.R.B.62

Spencer Street, looking up towards Briery Hill. This street is well known even to today's Ebbw Vale residents, owing to the fact that there was a Chinese laundry there, which can be seen to the right of the photograph. Note the gas lamp on the corner of the street, the gas for which was, at one time, supplied from the steel works. The view up Spencer Street now shows that the buildings on the right hand side have been demolished. The small car park is all that remains of the Palace Theatre.

Looking down Spencer Street. The spire of Christ Church can be seen from most parts of the town and outlying areas. The view down the hill shows Newtown in the distance; the high building to the left is Penuel the base for the local scout movement. Partially hidden behind the trees is Canolfan Ganu, which is home to the Ebbw Vale Male Voice Choir. This was the old Bethesda chapel in Church Street. Spencer Street linked Victoria Road with Briery Hill and together these areas formed the original town of Ebbw Vale.

The Tabernacle Chapel pictured here was replaced by a new building on Armoury Hill in 1908. This old building later became a Synagogue and was used by various organisations such as the Boys Brigade and St John's Ambulance Brigade. It was demolished to make way for the Briery Hill block of flats, seen in the second photograph during the 1960s.

A view from the Drysiog farm mountain gate on Briery Hill, showing the old iron works behind the church spire, with a view of Newtown. Newtown was a series of terraces that were built to accommodate workers from the ironworks and the brickyards, mainly Brynheulog brickworks. The spoil tips can be seen on the skyline. The present day photo shows the 'new' Newtown, the tips have now been landscaped, but there is still evidence of the old furnaces. Just to the right of the spire can be seen what was known as 45 yard. This was named after the cylinders of the original furnace, built there in 1846, which were 45in in diameter.

General View from Mountain Gate Ebbw Vale

CHURCH ST EBBW VALE

The top photo looking south from Church Street shows the Palace Cinema and the staff of the Bonanza - a major department store that was left gutted after a major fire on 3 April 1921. The owners relocated their business to Market Street where it became known as the Bargoed Emporium. It later became part of the George Rees and Jones Consortium. This street is a continuation of Victoria Road and between them catered for most of Ebbw Vale's shopping needs. The present day photo, again looking south, shows how the street has changed. There are very few shops now and some of the buildings are in need of repair.

The lower photo is looking north with the Bonanza with sunblinds, and on the opposite side of the road stands the Abercarn Shop. Some of these buildings have been given a new lease of life and have been converted into flats. It is worth noting how the facades of the shops in the two buildings have changed since being converted in to flats.

Church Street, Ebbw Vale.

The old telegraph and call office in Church Street (opposite the Institute) was built in 1900 and employed two counter staff, two telegram boys, a postman and postmaster. The bricks that formed the arch over the windows and decorative brickwork were made at the Beaufort Brickyard, to a size and scale specified by the builder. Looking at the present day it is possible to see that the decorative brickwork has been removed and, although the windows and doors are the same shape, the rest of the building is flat faced.

On 5 November 1849, a group of men met at the Old Penuel chapel. Their objective was, 'To make provision for the formation of classes of an educational and cultural character', and the holding of lectures on 'topical and technical' subjects. The manager of the steelworks at that time, Mr Thomas Brown, promised to erect a building to be used for this purpose. Work on the building was started in 1852 and was finished by 1853. It was named the Ebbw Vale Literary & Scientific Institute, or as it is commonly known 'The Stute'. It was recorded that 'borrowings from the library during the year was 350 volumes'. The main hall of the institute has been used for many purposes and for its first fifty years was the main social centre in the town. It has been used over the years to hold religious services and school and celebrity concerts. The main post office for the town was in the building until 1900, when it was transferred across the road to the telegraph and call office. It has also been home to the local constabulary and the main hall has been used as a police court. In 1894 it was requisitioned by the Military Authorities and used for the billeting of troops, who had been drafted into the town during the Rhondda Hauliers strike to offer protection to the miners of the town who refused to join in the strike. The Ebbw Vale Technical School was also housed in this building from 1931 until 1963. Just to the right of the doorway on the modern photograph is a water fountain that was cast in 1886 and in use at the bottom of Armoury Hill until 1930 when it was removed to make way for a public convenience.

The spire that can be seen belongs to the Tabernacle Chapel, which was built in 1908, to replace the building that had been used at Briery Hill. It remained as a chapel until 1982 when the land was used to build a sheltered housing complex that is known as Ty Penry Thomas. A point worth mentioning in the old photograph is the telegraph pole, which cannot be seen today as the telephone cables are mainly now underground. The road to the left is Eureka Place, and where the figures are standing, there is a road that goes up a steep hill to the Ebbw Vale hospital.

Chapter 2

ARMOURY HILL
TO BETHCAR
STREET

The Old Surgery at Armoury Terrace, which at one time was the main surgery for the town as there were some doctors who worked from their homes. Notice the long wall to the right of the photograph, which hid a feeder pond. The pond was filled in to provide ground for the building of parts of Armoury Terrace and Bethcar Street.

Some of the population waiting in the rain to welcome Prince Phillip when he visited the town on 18 July 1958. His visit coincided with the Commonwealth Games taking place in Cardiff. As can be seen in the new photograph a launderette and the Market Tavern have replaced part of the lower floor of the Bon Marché. The council offices were just behind the building on the left with the fire station a little further along the road.

On 19 June 1957 the park on the Drill Ground was used for the proclamation of the Royal National Eisteddfod to be held in Ebbw Vale in 1958. The stones for the Gorsedd circle were quarried at the Trefil Quarry. They were later removed to their present site near the council offices, owing to the park being excavated to make room for an extension to the steel works. At the National Eisteddfod at Rhyl in 1985 a local boy, Robert Powell, pictured right, was the first Welsh language learner to be crowned Bard. He was awarded the Bardic Chair for his entry entitled *Cynefin*. His Nom-de -Plume was Penycae, the old name for Ebbw Vale.

BON MARCHE, EBBW VALE.

The Bon Marché on Bethcar Street, with its sunblinds over the windows, was a department store that sold a large range and variety of goods. The building takes up approximately a third of the visible area of Bethcar Street. The present day photograph shows that the street has since seen pedestrianised. The upper floors of what was part of the Bon Marché have been converted into flats and the ground floor has become the indoor market.

This view of Bethcar Street looking north, and on the opposite side of the road to the Bon Marché, shows what life was like during the 1960s, with ample on street parking and wide pavements. Note the people waiting at the bus stop for the regular service bus. The present day picture shows the street from the opposite direction, with trees planted as part of the re-development as well as the pedestrianisation which took place in 1985. The spire of Christ Church can be seen in the distance.

A parade was held through the town on 19 June 1957 to celebrate the proclamation of the intention to hold the Royal National Eisteddfod at Ebbw Vale in 1958. The Astoria cinema can be seen at the top centre of the picture through the gap in the trees. The view is to the north along Bethcar Street towards the crossing. The present day photograph shows the same view on a Friday, which is a street market day.

Ebbw Vale is one of the valley towns that is over 1000ft above sea level and therefore can expect, and indeed receives some inclement weather, as can be seen from this photograph of Bethcar Street taken on 6 March 1965. The snow started to fall on Wednesday evening and the town was soon isolated, with no traffic moving until Friday. The town library can be seen on the left. It was purchased by the county council and converted from the old Bethcar chapel. Today's somewhat less snowy scene looks south from opposite the library.

During its history Ebbw Vale has had several police stations including this in Bethcar Street. This building still had a courthouse attached, as can be seen on the left of the picture. The old station was run by its sergeant, whose wife received payment for supplying the meals for the prisoners in the cells. When the old police station was being demolished and the new station was being built, the police station at Cwm became the centre of operations.

Some of the cinema goers at the White House Cinema, pictured in 1931, with Harold Lloyd and Constance Cummings who were promoting the film Movie Crazy. Woolworths stands on the site of the White House Cinema after the highly ornate building was demolished in 1958. Prior to the building of the new Woolworths stores, it was situated on the opposite side of the road between what was the Gas shop and Liptons.

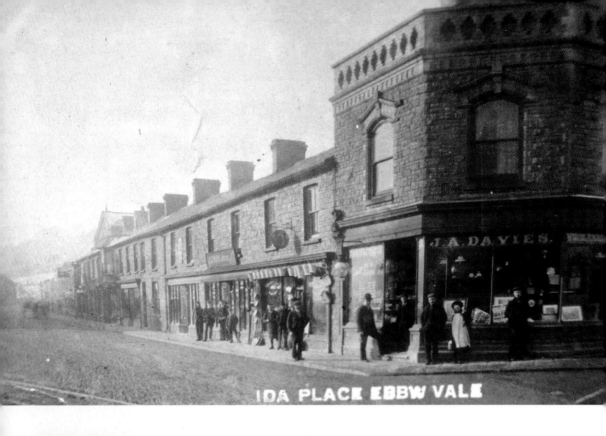

IDA PLACE EBBW VALE

Ida Place is a continuation of Bethcar Street and runs north from the library. At the bottom left of this photograph from the early 1900s the rails of The Crossing can be seen. The shop in the foreground was owned by J A Davies, who was a both a builder and builders merchant. The shop today is better known as May's, for ladies fashions although it has now changed hands and Phillip Haines, an estate agent, is based there. It is worth noting how although the buildings in the modern picture have changed a great deal at ground level, the buildings themselves changed very little.

West End Terrace pictured in the early 1900s, before the Workmen's Hall was built in 1907. The photograph shows the railway line that ran in front of the houses. The line ran behind Bethcar Street, in front of Eureka Place then through the tunnel to Brynheulog brickworks before ending at the Trefil quarry. The line was extended in 1858 to what is now Church Street to enable the transport of the stone used to build Christ Church, opened in 1861. The Workmen's Hall has had a varied history since its construction and has been used for concerts by artists including Tom Jones, as the Grenada cinema and as a bingo hall. The new photograph shows that the original houses remain and the outward appearance of the buildings have changed only slightly.

WEST END TER EBBW VALE

DEDICATION OF EBBW VALE WAR MEMORIAL

The dedication of the war memorial on 24 September 1924 at The Crossing, to which an estimated 10,000 people attended. The memorial was unveiled by Sir Frederick Mills, Chairman of the Ebbw Vale Iron and Steel Company Ltd. Rees Street can be seen in the background, with the building on the right, which is now home to the Principality Building Society, at the south end of James Street. On the upper left of the photo, opposite Rees Street, is the site of the Astoria Cinema, built in 1940. This was bought by Tesco in 1970 and used as a supermarket before being converted into The Picture House, a Wetherspoons pub. The memorial was re-sited at its present position in Libanus Road in 1950.

The war memorial on the crossing, showing the Weavers Tripe factory in between the Central garage and the butchers shop. The tripe factory was later moved to the rear of Pennant Street. The small brick building to the right of the picture was the shelter for the person in charge of the level crossing. He would come out of the building with a red flag in his hand to stop the traffic on the road and allow the trains to and from the brickworks to go past. The butchers shop is still open and is now in the hands of Noel Weston. The local offices of the Gwent Gazette are now on the upper floor of the building. The public conveniences, pictured behind the security van, are now situated on the site of the Central garage.

The War Memorial (3) Ebbw Vale. 277.

A drawing by Ron Francis, a local artist from Abertillery, of the original Ex Service men's club situated behind Market Street. The large cannons in the drawing were melted down for scrap during the Second World War. The present day photograph shows the well-maintained Ebbw Vale Ex-Servicemen's Club and Institute, just off the bypass road. It is known locally as The Dugout.

Chapter 3
MARKET STREET TO JAMES STREET AND GANTRE

Market Street looking south during the 1950s with Sidoli's café on the right of the picture. Sidoli is a long established ice cream manufacturer and has had a factory in the town for many years. The white building at the end of the street is the old Plaza Cinema. Today's view shows the café with white chairs outside it. The cafe has been renamed as The Crossing Café by its present owners.

A view of the Station car park around. 1970. This photograph was taken at a time of great upheaval in the town - after the closure of the LMS railway station and the removal of the shops that faced onto Market Street. The station was the High Level railway station in the centre of the town and was closed because of the redevelopment of the town centre. To the left of the photograph is where the multi-storey car p/ark is today. To the right on the first picture is the Bargoed Emporium, which is now Davies Wallpapers. Today's photograph gives the impression of being on a continental style Piazza with wide open spaces and tree lined streets. Note how the construction of the multi-storey car park has allowed the street to be pedestrianised.

Looking north from The Crossing during the 1960s, with the Catholic church at the end of James Street visible in the distance. The railway lines have been removed, the high level station has closed and a roundabout has replaced the War Memorial. Today's view shows that the multi-storey car park now dominates the skyline, although the Catholic church can still clearly be seen. When rebuilt by Tesco in 1970 the front of what is now The Picture House pub was brought forward in line with the front of James Street. To the left of the photograph can be seen May's Shop. This was owned by May Parry who was an outstanding pianist and was the accompanist for the Ebbw Vale Male Voice Choir.

Celebrations of the coronation of Queen Elizabeth II taking place outside the Plaza, c. 1953. The Plaza was opened in 1937 having been built on the site of the old market hall but was demolished in 1970 to make way for the town's bypass. This was one of four cinemas in the town that provided the main entertainment before television and it was not unusual to see queues waiting patiently in the rain to see the latest releases. Today's view shows the site of the Plaza, although since its construction in the 1970s this area has seen many changes in the road system and direction of traffic.

The County Hotel on Market Square. The photograph also shows the County Buildings and on the extreme left, Tredegar Road which crossed over the railway to the high level station by means of a stone bridge. Today's photograph shows very little change to the actual buildings with the main changes being to the road system which replaced a roundabout. This was done in preparation for the Garden Festival of Wales, which was held in 1992. The pedestrian controlled lights were added as a safety measure, due to the expected increase of traffic at the time.

Market Square from Market Street looking north, showing Libanus Chapel and the Market Hall to the right. It is worthwhile to compare the two facades of Libanus chapel. On the new picture an extension has been built onto the front of the original building. The modern view also shows how the multi-storey car park dominates the skyline.Daniel's has replaced the Market Hall on the right. Libanus Road was at one time the main road out of town.

The photograph taken from the Tredegar road bridge, which was demolished in the 1960s as part of the redevelopment, shows the old high level station in use, with James Street on the right and Market Street on the left. The other photograph shows the bridge after the railway ceased to function. The bridge frames the route of the new road that follows the route of the London Midland and Scottish Railway line, northward to the Heads of the Valleys Road. To the left of the picture is the Catholic Church while the swimming pool can be seen in the distance.

The multi-storey car park pictured while under construction, *c.* 1970. After the removal of the Tredegar Road Bridge and the railway station in 1970, the railway line was removed and a new road leading to the Heads of the Valley road was constructed. The multi-storey car park, together with some modern shops, was erected in the area where the Railway Station stood. Today's photograph shows there is a road junction where the Tredegar road bridge used to span the railway track.

Robert and Hetti Clubb pictured in James Street with two of their four daughters, Alice and Pat. Robert and Hetti also had four sons, all of whom originally lived in Lilian Grove. Mr Clubb received the MM during the First World War when he served with the South Wales Borderers on the Somme. While on patrol with his platoon, he was acting as a rearguard and was some distance behind the platoon. The platoon was ambushed and the sergeant in charge told his troops to lay down their weapons. Mr Clubb surprised the Germans and rescued his platoon. Mr Clubb was subsequently employed at the Marine Colliery for 53 years. During this time he had an industrial accident which resulted in his right leg being permanently straight. Their son Peter was well known in the 1950s as a centre for Ebbw Vale Rugby

Club. He later 'went north' to play rugby league for Wigan. The next photograph shows James Street as it is today, with the Co-operative chemist on the right and the multi-storey car park on the left. The high building in the centre of the background is the Picture House.

The distinctive L shape construction of the Gantre cottages can be seen here. Built around 1810 to house workmen employed at the Gantre pit, the lower floor was below road level. The Gorsedd circle stones are now standing on the site of the cottages, after being removed from the Drill ground owing to the expansion of the steel works. Further developments of the Glyncoed area can also be seen in the photograph including the fire station and Glycoed housing estate.

The Gantre cottages can be seen just above the houses in this picture of Beaufort Road. The Sychffos terrace houses can be seen to the left of the photograph, along with the tips just above the cemetery. The tips were later removed. The present day photograph shows the amount of change that has taken place. The houses in the foreground still exist as does cemetery but also visible are the Glyncoed estate, a new fire station and the Gwent Tertiary College. It is also worth noting how much vegetation has returned to the hillsides, due to the lack of industrial pollution.

eaufort Road Ebbw Vale.

This patch of wasteground was once site of the Sychffos, a row of terrace houses built in 1814 that were demolished under the general re-housing scheme. The view is from the Valley Road area looking towards the new fire station, some time during the 1960s. Tesco now uses the site for its new supermarket.

Chapter 4

LIBANUS CORNER

AND

NEWTOWN

A view of Libanus corner showing one of Offie Edmunds buses, that were considered to be one of the 'institutions' of the time. Even though the company usually bought second hand buses, it provided excellent local services, often still running when other bus companies failed due to the inclement weather. Today the traffic is controlled by a large traffic island.

A view of Pontygof from around 1890 showing the infants school where the War Memorial is today. Also to be seen are the G.W.R station, the Big Arch and the smokestacks of the original iron works below Newtown. The road to the right of the school is Libanus Road. The tip in the foreground of the picture has been planted with potatoes. The present day scene is far removed from the earlier photograph, as many of the buildings, and the railway, no longer exist.

One of the regular carnivals that used to be held in the town, with a large number of children in fancy dress making its way over the old railway bridge towards the welfare grounds. Colliers Row and Western Terrace can also be seen. The building on the left is at the end of Bridge Street and is now the site of the health centre. The present day view shows the traffic island at Libanus corner and the health centre.

The carnival parade in June 1963, pictured near the council offices. This was one of the highlights of the year and was well supported by the local population. It is perhaps a sign of the times when thirty-seven years later it appears that carnivals no longer play a part in the lives of the local community. The large traffic island in the new picture replaced the five road junctions to ease the flow of traffic to the Ebbw Vale steelworks to the left, and to the town centre via Libanus Road on the right. The road itself has been relegated from what was the main road out of town, to a secondary class road which mainly serves the council offices, Crown buildings and leisure centre. After this it continues on until joining up again with the new road from the town.

The Lido, which was to the north of the present day rugby field and opposite the Beaufort Arms. It was built in May 1930 by a body of unemployed men who offered to build a new outdoor swimming pool, without payment. Prior to this the only means of swimming was to create a dam across the river Ebbw. The Lido was closed in 1961. The River Ebbw has diverted its course over the years and remains of the Lido can be seen at the riverbank. An indoor swimming pool was built in 1962 by the local authority, on the site of the Gantre tip area. This was the first building of the new leisure complex.

Ebbw Vale's Lido

The Arch, Ebbw Vale.

M.J.R.B. 629

A timber arch was built in 1813 to carry the raw materials for the furnaces in the 45 yard. The present stone arch replaced this in 1869 and at the time the road was the main road from Ebbw Vale to Tyllwyn and Waunlwyd. The pedestrian tunnel was added as a safety measure, owing to the large increase in traffic. The road under the arch is now only used for access to the area known as the Crescent. It is possible to see that although these photographs are around 100 years apart, the paint splashes on the brickwork are still the same.

The GWR Bridge was built in 1813, at the same time as the original Big Arch. This was the main railway line from Ebbw Vale travelling south, serving both the town works and the valley communities to Newport. The line was closed in the 1960s and parts of the track bed were removed and replaced by a new road. The stonework on the left is all that remains of the old road bridge that crossed the railway. The main road now runs through this arch.

Great Western Ra—
Ebbw Vale

Artwork of the GWR Station at Ebbw Vale by Michael Blackmore, a local artist from Abertillery. This shows the location of the Gantre tips on the top left, and the Bridge End hotel, which is adjacent to the welfare ground. The present day photo still shows the Bridge End hotel and, almost hidden behind the trees, the new stand at the Eugene Cross Park, formerly the Welfare ground. The council offices can be seen on top left of the picture where the Gantre tip once stood. Reflecting its connection to the railway, the new road follows the route of the old railway track and the houses on right are known as Station Approach.

An early aerial view of the 45 yard furnaces. At the top centre of the photograph, just below Newtown, is Louvain Terrace. On closer inspection the railway network that serviced the furnaces can be seen while at the bottom of the picture is Big House - the home of the works owners. The general office is on the right. Today's view is from the area above the furnaces, where the railway wagons were taken to be unloaded directly into the furnaces. From there they returned to the works or to the quarry; via the embankment over the top of the Big Arch and the GWR Arch.

The first four rows of Newtown were built as workmen's cottages for the men employed at the iron works while the other three rows were used by workers at the brickwork's. These also became subject to the re-housing scheme and were demolished in the 1960s when new houses were built on the same site. The Britannia Inn, built during the 1830s or 40s, is the only building left standing on the site and is one of the oldest buildings in the town. It is still in use as a public house even today.

Aneurin 'Nye' Bevan, M.P for Ebbw Vale from 1929 until 1960, at the inauguration of the Sir William Firth Gates at the Welfare ground on 29 April 1959. Also in the photograph is Sir Eugene Cross MBE, MM, JP; whom the ground was re-named after in 1974. . Nye Bevan was the mastermind behind the National Health Service and introduced it on 5 July 1948 to a grateful nation, still reeling from the after effects of the Second World War. Sir Eugene was the chairman of Trustees of the Ebbw Vale Miners Welfare Association for many decades. The association was originally set up so that amateur sportsmen and sportswomen could use the grounds. Today's

photograph shows how the ground is now home to the professional rugby fraternity.

A photograph of the Welfare ground and old stands, showing the original floodlight system in the late 1950s. To the left of the stand is a footpath that came down to the Welfare ground after crossing over the railway bridge from Libanus Corner. To the right of the stand is the railway goods shed. The deliveries from this were made with a Three-wheeled Scammell, a vehicle that was used extensively by British Rail. One of the last drivers of these vehicles to be employed at this depot was Jack Ford, a man well known and respected in gardening circles. He was transferred to Merthyr Tydfil after the closure of the line. In the background the council offices can be seen. The present day shows the leisure centre has joined the council offices on the skyline while a new stand has been built and the goods shed has long since been demolished during the 1960s.

A view from the council offices during the 1960s, at a time when the seven rows of houses in Newtown had been demolished as part of the re-housing scheme. The Welfare ground with its two stands can be seen in the foreground, as can Pontygof School, which was was built in 1848 by the Ebbw Vale Iron and Steel and Coal Company. The Britannia Pub, the large building in the distance, can be seen casting a solitary eye over the, temporary, desolation. Today's photograph shows that the stand on the right has now been transformed into the clubhouse while the old school has gone, to be replaced with a modern building, hidden among the trees.

The indoor swimming pool was built in 1962 and was considered by many people to be the best swimming pool in Wales. Today's view from the Civic Centre shows the additions of a leisure centre in 1972 while the Hydroslides were an addition in 1994. Note all the other building developments in the outlying areas that have replaced the fields. To the left of the photograph is the new Tesco stores, top left can be seen the comprehensive school and the Gwent Tertiary College, renamed Goleg Gwent. Also visible are the new industrial estates and the Rassau housing estate which is sited to the north of town. The new road into Ebbw Vale can be seen on the left.

Chapter 5
WILLOWTOWN TO
BEAUFORT HILL

The Gantre brickworks adjacent to Valley Road. This was one of two such brickworks, the other being Brynheulog, the chimneys of which can be seen at the top of the photograph. The railway line in the foreground led from the Trefil Quarry to the steelworks. The feeder pond has been filled and is now a children's play area, while the main building was used by a haulage contractor before it was demolished. It is now a green and pleasant recreational area used by all of the local inhabitants.

WILLOW TOWN, EBBW VALE.

Mount Pleasant Road in the Willowtown area, The first photograph was taken from the top of a spoil tip, which came from the various pits in the immediate area. This shows the approach from the north and at the front left can be seen where excavations had been made possibly for coal removal. In the centre on the left the farm on Hughes' Avenue can be seen. Centre right in prominent view is Mount Pleasant Chapel, one of the few chapels of the era that is still going strong. In the next photo the tips are gone giving a slightly different view of the road. The excavations have been filled in and Monwel Hankinson, who mainly employ disabled persons in the manufacture of roadsigns, now uses the site. There are also new houses to the right and trees are again growing where once there was only the remains of industry.

Ebbw Vale County Grammar School pictured from the front gate on Beaufort Road around 1912. Bronwydd, the home of Mr W A Jones, clerk to the council around this time, is on the far right of the photo. The original school building was known as 'the old block' in latter years, after a new block was added in 1936. A new science block and assembly hall was built in 1962. The school was renamed Glanyrafon Comprehensive School under re-organisation in 1975 before it closed in July 1999. There has been no decision as to the further use that can be made of the buildings and the school now stands unused.

N orth Monmouthshire College of Further Education in the Waun -y -Pound area pictured during the early 1970s. This was opened in 1962 and later became the Gwent Tertiary College. It is a place where all age groups may go to improve on their education or to re-train for a new direction in their working life.

During the build up to the
Commonwealth Games in Cardiff in
1958 the Queen's message was sent
throughout Wales. The honour of carrying
it in the Ebbw Vale Area fell to Jim
Holland and Ray Caswell. The
photograph shows them on the run from
the top of Sirhowy Hill towards the Rhyd-
y-Blew on 18 July, with the official car
behind them. Being typical of the
youngsters of the day, they still found time
to have a joke. It has been said that one
asked the other, 'What would happen if we
threw it into the Waun-y-Pound pond as
we passed by, or if we turned left and ran
over the moors?' To which the reply was,
'I don't think we should because that guy
in the car is likely to shoot us'. Note the
railway viaduct that was known as the

seven arches, that was later demolished to
make way for the approach road to town
from the Heads of the Valley road.
Although the viaduct has gone the scene has
changed comparatively little over the years.

During the snowfall of March 1947 a train at Beaufort station became snowbound in the platform and was there for several days before it could be removed, as there apparently was not enough coal left to re-light the fire. The ballroom can be seen on the right. In the modern, slightly warmer looking, photograph it is possible to see where the railway has been filled in. Private housing now occupies the ground where the railway lines used to run. The ballroom is still in place and is regularly used for quality performances by local dramatic societies and well-known artists.

Beaufort Junior Hill School (1874-1991) situated on the A467 road between Beaufort and Brynmawr can be seen in the centre of the photograph. The present day view shows the main road to the left of the photograph while the site of the school is just beyond the bend in the road. The area has been well developed since the early photograph with Frost road to the right and Park Hill Estate, built during the 1960s, to be seen between the electricity pylons.

During the early hours of 26 March 1995 a fire broke out which gutted the main building of the old Beaufort Hill Junior School. Six fire engines attended, the road was closed and thirty-five firemen battled to control the blaze. The second photograph shows the aftermath of the fire and the unsafe building that had to be demolished. The site has since been used to build twenty-eight new homes. The new Beaufort Hill Primary School opened in 1991 adjacent to the Pen-y-Cwm special school, which is near the Parkhill Estate.

Beaufort Municipal theatre was opened in March 1961 and was an extension to the previous building that housed the ballroom. This view shows the seating arrangements of the theatre, which can seat up to 417 patrons. The building is at present being renovated and refurbished as part of the Valleys Roots Project, a scheme to promote the arts in the valleys. Here the main sports hall of the Ebbw Vale Leisure Centre, built in 1972 as a multi-purpose centre, is in set up for use as a concert hall. Since 1994 it has been called the Beaufort Theatre and Ballroom and received an Arts Council of Wales Lottery award in 1997 for alterations and upgrading to be carried out, It now has seating for 360 and is one of fourteen Arts Council for Wales Core venues.

A presentation was made to C.S.M Jack Williams; V.C, D.C.M, M.M, Croix de Guerre; at Briery Hill School in 1920. Richard Thomas and Baldwins, who owned the steel works prior to nationalisation, employed Mr Williams at the general offices as a Commisionaire. By comparison, today's photograph shows the children of Glyncoed Junior School at the 1995 celebrations of V.E Day. The school, which opened in 1939, celebrated its 60th anniversary last year with a Second World War exhibition of wartime memorabilia.

Mr Joe Richards, headmaster of Pontygof school, pictured during the early 1940s. He was educated at Ebbw Vale County School, then went to the Monmouthshire Training College at Caerleon for training as a teacher. During the First World War he served in the administration branch of the Royal Navy. After the war he represented Ebbw Vale at cricket for 17 years, captained a successful hockey team and also played tennis and golf. He was on the staff of Pontygof School for 25 years. His hobbies were angling, shooting, and natural history and he frequently lectured on these subjects as well as having various articles published. Mrs Williams the new head of the modern day infants and primary school pictured dealing with the complexities of modern

school administration. The original school was pulled down in 1975 and was replaced by the junior section that same year. The new infants' section in opened in 1985.

On many occasions people of various callings have visited the town and they all left with their own impression of the town and surrounding areas. One of these impressions is the painting of the Morning Star public house by Obediah Hodges in 1907. As can be seen, Mr Hodges has used a certain amount of artistic license. The second photo shows a present day view from a similar viewpoint. The Morning Star is now a private dwelling house.

Chapter 6

EBBW VALE

STEELWORKS

The weekly edition of The Times newspaper from Thursday, 21 July 1938, showing an artist's impression of the rolling mills at the steelworks. This was an important time for Ebbw Vale, where true to previous form, parts of the old works were demolished to make way for the New Works - including the building of the cold mill. The transformation started in 1937 and took approximately 15 months to complete. This came at the time when the country was preparing for conflict with the Axis powers and as a result more men were needed to man the furnaces and to process the steel. The works was running night and day producing high-grade steel and because of this the town and surrounding areas prospered.

The old general offices, which were the nerve centre of the works, seen here around the turn of the century. They were built near to the 45 yard to be close to the works and to give ready access to the managers house which was situated between the general office and the works. The present building was built around the old offices, so that there would not be any interruption to production control during the re-build. The clock, which was once on the top of a chapel in Augusta Street in the Victoria area, bears the inscription, 'Time floeth away without delay,' and is dated 1916. The second photograph shows the new general offices and part of the culvert system taking the River Ebbw underneath the works.

A photograph from the Times' feature on the Ebbw Vale works' reconstruction entitled 'A Marvellous transformation. The view shows the site in preparation for the construction of the Cold Mill in April 1937.

This picture dates from around 15 months later and is again from the same Times' feature. This view shows the works from a different angle as the construction work nears completion.

Here men can be seen levelling the ground outside the Hot Mill during the reconstruction. In the background the massive blast furnaces can be seen.

The bright lights of the works pierce the gloom of the night as the coke ovens continues burning through the night in 1969. Within twelve months of this photograph being taken the run down of the steel industry would be announced.

In 1960 Llanwern steelworks near Newport was opened, and gradually the works started to run down its production. Skilled men were transferred to Llanwern to work in the steel plant and other departments of the works. Over the years less and less steel was produced at Ebbw vale and the works concentrated on rolling tinplate, until the decision was made to stop iron and steel production completely. Here the coal bunker is pictured being demolished in 1979.

The demolition of the blast furnaces in 1979. The rundown of the steel industry was announced in 1970.

The Coke ovens and by-product plant closed in 1971, followed by the closure of the blast furnaces and steel making plant in 1975. Shown here is the demolition of the gas holder.

Ironically the Rt Hon Michael Foot, MP for Ebbw Vale from 1960 to 1992, became Secretary of State for Employment in 1974 and received a hostile reception when he announced the closure of steelmaking in Ebbw Vale. Seen here are the demolition of the coal blenders in 1979.

Very few of the industries reliant on the steelworks remain in Ebbw Vale, although both tinplating and steel finishing remain. Pictured here are the the demolition of the cooling towers in 1979.

The demolition of the open hearth in 1979.

The site of the south end of the steelworks pictured in August 1987. After the demolition of the steel making plants, local campaigners and councillors fought hard to ensure that the site of the steelworks would not end up as a permanent scar on the landscape. The focus of their campaign was that the town should be host to a garden festival on the site of the steelworks. The campaigners got their wish and the garden festival came into being in 1992. The festival site is still open today, on a reduced scale, with visitors returning to see the garden displays and sights, visit the festival shopping centre and remember the good times they had.

Victoria Road showing the Goliath cranes that handled the iron ore, before it went to the furnaces. The disused old road can be seen on the left. The route of the new road takes it passes through what was part of the old steelworks and leads up past Garden City. This part of town was unfortunate as residents had the coke ovens of the steelworks on their doorstep. The coke ovens were where the coal was burned slowly to remove the various sulphurs and tars that would interfere with the quality of iron from the blast furnace. This led to large amounts of pollutants in the air around the ovens.

The south-gate, or as it was known to the workers 'the heavy end' because of the nature of the work in this part of the plant compared to the lighter work at the other end. The photograph shows the steel making plant, with the security office and the timekeepers office on the left and the surgery and bathhouse on the right. The security staffs are known by the name of 'spotters'. This does not stem from their watching of the workers but because during the First World War some of them were sent to the top of the local mountain to act as 'aircraft spotters' in the event of a bomber raid on the works. The works also had gates at the north, east and west approaches, with the east and west gates used mainly for pedestrian access. The second photograph shows the view today with the south gate now just a roundabout and junction.

The old Caersalem chapel in Victoria, built in 1839, was demolished in December 1936 to make way for the new steelworks extensions. The Victoria Institute building, near the south gate of the steelworks became its home from 1936 to 1952. This building can be seen in the background under the furl of the banner. The new building of the Caersalem Baptist Church Waunlwyd held it's opening service on 28 June 1952. It was built by voluntary labour during 1949 and 1950 and is on an embankment opposite the Park Hotel and near to the steelworks road. Greenery has now taken over from the mainly industrial scene.

Chapter 7
WAUNLWYD TO
CWM

An artist's impression of Ebbw Vale by renowned artist L.S Lowry called Hillside in Wales. This painting can be seen hanging in the Tate Gallery in London. Lowry stayed in Ebbw Vale with the family of Mrs Barbara Evans in 1958, when he judged the art competition at the National Eisteddfod. He made sketches of the local area at the time that he used in the final painting, depicting his impression of the Victoria area. Of Victoria and its many terraces only the two houses in the background remain.

The shop in the centre of the photograph was the first Industrial and Provident Society in the area and opened on Thursday 17 April 1902 at Station Road in Waunlwyd. The shop soon had a membership of 371 with sales of £7,875, with a share loan; small savings capital of £932 and reserves of £28. By 1948 this had risen to 5961 members and had sales totalling £432,031 and share, loan and small savings capital as £304,396 with reserves of £15,123. It also had investments of £295,990. The second photograph shows that the only remaining buildings are Park Hotel and what is known as the 'BIG House', built for the manager of Waunlwyd colliery. Station Road was demolished to make way for the new road improvements. This area has at least benefited from the closure of the

lower end of the steelworks. Buildings no longer receive the coatings of red dust and dropout of material from the works and is now a pleasant place to live, with views over the site of the Garden Festival of Wales.

The first photograph was taken from the site of the Waunlwyd colliery after the line was closed to passenger traffic. The south end of the steelworks, destined for demolition, can be seen in the distance. The next photograph shows the scene as it is today and is a good example of the way that nature has recovered. The grass and trees are thriving and and have returned a once industrial wasteland into the green and pleasant land it was many years ago.

A view of Waunlwyd Colliery in 1970, prior to its demolition in 1974. Cwm Road can be seen along with the allotments behind the houses. The nearest row of houses on Cwm Road was demolished to build the new road. The building in the bottom left corner of the old photograph is situated approximately where the Festival shopping centre is today. The photograph shows the new housing that has been built on the site of the old colliery with the Cwm Road above it.

Waunlwyd Colliery, sunk in 1874, showing two saddle tank engines on the main line and a quantity of railway wagons in the sidings, waiting to be loaded. The present day picture shows the great changes in the area with only a single track in operation and the houses of the new housing estate on the site, where the colliery once stood. It is hoped that Ebbw Vale will eventually see the return of a passenger train service to the eastern and western valleys.

The Lime plant was where the steelworks' limestone was burned to make lime for the furnaces and was situated opposite Waunlwyd. The lime was used to remove impurities from the iron and steel. The photograph of this area taken during the garden festival shows the rainbow created from flowers, some of the various attractions and the hothouse. The hothouse is one of the many parts of the festival site that has been maintained today. The old sign for Waunlwyd Colliery can be seen to this day.

Troed-Rhiw-Clawdd farm, situated above and to the left of the lime-plant, can be seen above the slag tips to the left of centre in the photograph. An old legend surrounds the stone in one of Troed-Rhiw-Clawdd's fields. An old man and his wife lived at the farm when he became ill during a blizzard. He died within a week and his wife was left with no option but to salt the body and wait until the blizzard finished two weeks later. She hailed a passing shepherd and they dug a grave to bury the salted corpse. They rolled a large stone over the crude grave and the stone can be seen to this day. The second photograph shows Prince Charles on the occasion of the opening of Garden Festival Wales on the 5 May 1992. Here he is seen meeting farmer Wyndham Morris, one of 19 children, who lives at Troed-Rhiw-Clawdd farm.

A view from the A4046 at the south end of garden festival site showing the start of the land reclamation in 1986. The Garden Festival bid was made by Blaenau Gwent Borough Council in 1985. In November 1986 the Welsh Secretary Nicholas Edwards MP, announced that Ebbw Vale was to hold the fifth and last National Garden Festival. The tips in the photograph were the result of many years of depositing molten slag from the steelworks. 142 acres of derelict land was reclaimed, with many thousands of tons of material having to be removed. The next photograph shows the view from Cwm cemetery road after the opening of the Garden Festival Wales in 1992 with the many varied attractions there.

Cwmyrdderch mixed school, situated just north of the railway station, pictured during the early 1900s. The early origins and buildings of Canning Street can be seen in the foreground of the photograph. Note the old farm in the location of present day Curre Street. The present day general view shows the flats that replaced the school, together with the houses that have been built on what was farmland.

The Marine Colliery, opened in 1891 by the Ebbw Vale Steel and Iron Company Ltd, pictured in April 1989 on the day the announcement was made to close the colliery. One of the tragedies that befell this colliery during its history was on Tuesday 1 March 1927 when an explosion underground claimed the lives of 52 mineworkers. The site of the colliery was cleared after the closure and the pit shaft was capped and marked by two halves of a winding wheel set in concrete. The site of the colliery was used as an overflow car park for the garden festival in 1992, when a park and ride system operated for the duration of the event.

Augusta Street, pictured in 1957 was part of the Victorian area, built between 1836 and 1840 and named after Queen Victoria. Because of the area's close proximity to the coke ovens of the steelworks the houses wore the grime that came from the oven's fumes. Victoria was demolished in the late 1950s but the road remains as the approach road to the Festival shopping centre. The second photograph shows the Garnllydan housing estate which was built to the north of the town as part of the re-housing project.

Queen Street, pictured below in 1957 was also near to the works and therefore received its fair share grime and dust. Although many of the inhabitants were reluctant to leave the area for the hitherto unknown housing estates of Hilltop, Garnlydan and Rassau, it was generally agreed that conditions had to be improved. The second photograph shows the Hilltop estate shortly after its construction in 1957.

The attempt to improve the living conditions of the residents of the town of Ebbw Vale and surrounding areas resulted in the housing project of the late 1950s. As a close knit community, that would not be separated from their neighbours, many of the residents of Victoria were re-housed at the new housing estates at Garnlydan, Rassau and Hilltop.